WUDU AND SALAH

Ablution and Daily Prayers
WUDU AND SALAH

TUGHRA
BOOKS

New Jersey

Written by
Orhan Sezgin

Art Director
Engin Çiftci

Illustrated by
Öznur Kalender

Published by Tughra Books
335 Clifton Ave., Clifton,
NJ, 07011, USA
www.tughrabooks.com

ISBN: 978-1-59784-286-0

1- INTENTION

Say: "I intend to make *wudu* for the sake of Allah."

2- WASHING THE HANDS

Wash both of your hands up to your wrists. Make sure that the water goes between your fingers.

3- WASHING THE MOUTH

Take water into your mouth three times, using your right hand. Rinse your mouth well each time before spitting out the water.

4- WASHING THE NOSE

Take water slowly up your nostrils by sniffing, three times, using your right hand. Clear your nose using your left hand.

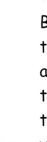

5- WASHING THE FACE

Bring your hands together and use a handful of water to wash your face three times from your forehead to the bottom of your chin, and then along the sides up to your ears.

6- WASHING YOUR RIGHT ARM

Wash your right arm, up to and including your elbow, three times.

7- WASHING YOUR LEFT ARM

Wash your left arm, up to and including your elbow, three times.

8- WIPING YOUR HEAD

Wet your right hand, and wipe at least a fourth of your head with it.

9- WIPING YOUR EARS

Wet your hands and wipe the inside of your ears with the tips of the little finger, and wipe the back of your ears from bottom to top with your thumbs.

10-WIPING THE NAPE OF YOUR NECK

Wipe the nape and the sides of your neck with the back of your wet hands.

11-WASHING YOUR RIGHT FOOT

Wash your right foot, including the ankle, with the help of your left hand. Make sure that the water goes between your toes.

12-WASHING YOUR LEFT FOOT

Wash your left foot, including the ankle, with the help of your left hand. Make sure that the water goes between your toes.

AFTER *WUDU* YOU CAN:

read the Qur'an

perform the daily prayers

do your daily activities

circumambulate the Ka'ba

fall asleep lying down

lose consciousness

laugh while praying
so that someone else
hears you

go to the toilet or
pass wind

bleed, or if pus flows
from a cut or sore

vomit a mouthful
or more

1. Face the *qibla* (the direction of the Holy Mosque, the Ka'ba in Mecca) in a clean place and make your intention to pray.

2. Start the prayer by saying "*Allahu akbar*" (Allah is the greatest) and clasp your hands. Recite "Subhana-ka", "Al-Fatiha" and another *surah* such as "Al-Ikhlas" or "Al-Kauthar."

13

3. Then bow down saying "*Allahu akbar.*" Say "*Subhana Rabbiya'l-Azim*" (Glory be to My Lord, the Greatest) three times.

4. And then standing upright again, say these words: "*Sami'Allahu liman hamidah*" (Allah hears any who are thankful to Him). Do not clasp your hands while standing.

5. Then prostrate yourself, putting your forehead and nose to the floor, saying "*Allahu akbar.*" Our palms are on the floor and our head is between our hands. Say "*Subhana Rabbiyal A'la*" (Glory to My Lord, the Highest) three times when you put your forehead on the ground. Then, sit upright, saying "*Allahu akbar,*" and prostrate again.

Say "*Subhana Rabbiyal A'la*" (Glory to My Lord, the Highest) three times.

6. After prostrating yourself twice rise again to stand. Recite "Al-Fatiha" and another *surah* such as "Al-Ikhlas" or "Al-Kauthar" while clasping your hands.

Then bow down, stand upright again, and prostrate your-self again. When in a sitting position, offer the prayer of "At-Tahiyyatu." If you perform a two-unit daily prayer, then after "At-Tahiyyatu" offer the prayers "Allahumma Salli - Allahumma Barik," and "Rabbana."

8. Then turn your face to the right and the left, in turn, looking down at your shoulder and saying "*As-salamu alaykum wa-rahmatullah*" (May the peace and mercy of Allah be upon you) **each time.**

16

PERFORMING A FOUR-UNIT *SALAH*

1

After performing two units, offer the prayer of "At-Tahiyyatu" in the sitting position. Then sit up again.

2

Recite "Al-Fatiha" and another surah such as "Al-Ikhlas" or "Al-Kauthar" in the third and fourth units.

3

In the fourth unit, offer the prayers "Allahumma Salli-Barik," and "Rabbana" after "At-Tahiyyatu."

4

After offering these prayers, turn your face to the right and the left, in turn, looking down at your shoulder and saying "*As-salamu alaykum wa-rahmatullah*" (May the peace and mercy of Allah be upon you) each time.

5

If you perform a four-unit *fard* prayer, recite only "Al-Fatiha" in the third and fourth units.

6

When you perform the four-unit *sunnah* parts of the afternoon (*asr*) and night prayers (*isha*), offer the prayers "Allahumma Salli-Barik" after "At-Tahiyyat" while sitting in the second unit.

7

When you perform the *witr* prayer, raise your hands to your ears, saying "*Allahu akbar*", in the third unit after reciting "Al-Fatiha" and some additional verses. Then clasp your hands again to offer the prayers of "Qunut." After offering the prayers of *Qunut*, bow down saying "*Allahu akbar.*"

17

HOW MANY TIMES DO WE PRAY A DAY?

We perform *fard* prayers five times a day. They are as follows:

Early morning prayer (*Fajr* prayer)
Two units *sunnah* / Two units *fard*

Noon prayer (*Zuhr* prayer)
This is made up of ten units; the first group of four is the *sunnah* prayer, followed by a group of four units, the *fard* prayer, and another group of two that makes up another *sunnah* prayer.

Afternoon prayer (*Asr* prayer)
Four units *sunnah* / Four units *fard*

Evening prayer (*Maghrib* prayer)
The first group of three is the *fard* prayer and the other group of two is the *sunnah* prayer.
(In the *maghrib* prayer, the three-unit *fard* is performed before the two-unit *sunnah*).

Night prayer (*Isha* prayer)
It is made up of thirteen units; the first group of four is the *sunnah* prayer, followed by a group of four units, the *fard* prayer, and another group of two that makes up another *sunnah* prayer, and the last group of three that is the *witr* prayer.

YOUR *SALAH* IS CANCELLED IF YOU:

talk while praying

eat or drink

turn your chest away from the direction of the Ka'ba

laugh

sleep

lift your two feet at the same time while prostrating yourself

Remember that if you lose *wudu* while praying, your *salah* is also cancelled. You must begin again after *wudu*.

WHAT ARE THE OTHER PRAYERS BESIDE THE DAILY PRAYERS?

- The *tarawih* prayer is performed after every *isha* (night) prayer in the month of Ramadan only.

- Friday (*jumuah*) prayer is performed in congregation. It is performed at the same time as (and instead of) the *zuhr* (noon) prayer.

- There are also *eid* prayers offered during the two religious festivals of *Eid al-fitr* (celebrated at the end of the month of Ramadan) and *Eid al-adha* (the Feast of the Sacrifice).

- *Qada* prayer: Performing only the *fard* parts of daily prayers after missing them unintentionally.

- *Janazah* (funeral) prayer, performed after someone dies.

- *Awwabin* prayer is performed after evening prayer.

- *Tahajjud* prayer is performed at night.

- *Hajah* prayer is performed as a supplication.

- *Travel* prayer is performed during travel.

- *Kusuf* and *khusuf* prayer during the solar and lunar eclipses.

- *Tasbih* prayer is performed as a supplication.

SURAH AL-FATIHA

بِسْمِ اللهِ الرَّحْمَنِ الرَّحِيمِ

❂ اَلْحَمْدُ للهِ رَبِّ الْعَالَمِينَ ❂

اَلرَّحْمَنِ الرَّحِيمِ ❂ مَالِكِ يَوْمِ الدِّينِ

❂ اِيَّاكَ نَعْبُدُ وَاِيَّاكَ نَسْتَعِينُ

❂ اِهْدِنَا الصِّرَاطَ الْمُسْتَقِيمَ

صِرَاطَ الَّذِينَ أَنْعَمْتَ عَلَيْهِمْ غَيْرِ

❂ الْمَغْضُوبِ عَلَيْهِمْ وَلَا الضَّالِّينَ

1.1. In the name of Allah, the All-Merciful, the All-Compassionate

1.2. All praise and gratitude are for Allah, the Lord of the worlds,

1.3. The All-Merciful, the All-Compassionate,

1.4. The Master of the Day of Judgment.

1.5. You alone do We worship, and from You alone do we seek help.

1.6. Guide us to the Straight Path,

1.7. The Path of those whom You have favored, not of those who have incurred (Your) wrath, nor of those who are astray.

SURAH AL-FIL

بِسْمِ اللهِ الرَّحْمٰنِ الرَّحِيمِ

اَلَمْ تَرَ كَيْفَ فَعَلَ رَبُّكَ بِاَصْحَابِ الْفِيلِ ۞ اَلَمْ يَجْعَلْ كَيْدَهُمْ فِى تَضْلِيلٍ ۞ وَاَرْسَلَ عَلَيْهِمْ طَيْرًا اَبَابِيلَ ۞ تَرْمِيهِمْ بِحِجَارَةٍ مِنْ سِجِّيلٍ ۞ فَجَعَلَهُمْ كَعَصْفٍ مَأْكُولٍ ۞

In the name of Allah, the All-Merciful, the All-Compassionate

105.1. Have you considered how your Lord dealt with the people of the Elephant?

105.2. Did He not bring their evil scheme to nothing?

105.3. He sent down upon them flocks of birds (unknown in the land),

105.4. Shooting them with bullet-like stones of baked clay;

105.5. And so He rendered them like a field of grain devoured and trampled.

SURAH AL-QURAISH

بِسْمِ اللهِ الرَّحْمٰنِ الرَّحِيمِ

لِاِيلَافِ قُرَيْشٍ ۞ اِيلَافِهِمْ رِحْلَةَ الشِّتَاءِ وَالصَّيْفِ ۞ فَلْيَعْبُدُوا رَبَّ هٰذَا الْبَيْتِ ۞ الَّذِى اَطْعَمَهُمْ مِنْ جُوعٍ وَاٰمَنَهُمْ مِنْ خَوْفٍ ۞

In the name of Allah, the All-Merciful, the All-Compassionate

106.1. (At least) for favor of concord and security to the Quraysh,

106.2. Their concord and security in their winter and summer journeys,

106.3. Let them worship the Lord of this House (the Ka'ba),

106.4. Who has provided them with food against hunger, and made them safe from fear.

SURAH AL-MA'UN

بِسْمِ اللهِ الرَّحْمٰنِ الرَّحِيمِ

اَرَاَيْتَ الَّذِى يُكَذِّبُ بِالدِّيْنِ ۞ فَذٰلِكَ الَّذِى يَدُعُّ الْيَتِيْمَ ۞ وَلَا يَحُضُّ عَلٰى طَعَامِ الْمِسْكِيْنِ ۞ فَوَيْلٌ لِّلْمُصَلِّيْنَ ۞ اَلَّذِيْنَ هُمْ عَنْ صَلَاتِهِمْ سَاهُوْنَ ۞ اَلَّذِيْنَ هُمْ يُرَآؤُنَ ۞ وَيَمْنَعُوْنَ الْمَاعُوْنَ ۞

In the name of Allah, the All-Merciful, the All-Compassionate
107.1. Have you considered one who denies the Last Judgment?
107.2. That is he who repels the orphan,
107.3. And does not urge the feeding of the destitute.
107.4. And woe to those worshippers (denying the Judgment),
107.5. Those who are unmindful in their Prayers,
107.6. Those who want to be seen and noted (for their acts of worship),
107.7. Yet deny all assistance (to their fellowmen).

SURAH AL-KAUTHAR

بِسْمِ اللهِ الرَّحْمٰنِ الرَّحِيمِ

اِنَّا اَعْطَيْنٰكَ الْكَوْثَرَ ۞ فَصَلِّ لِرَبِّكَ وَانْحَرْ ۞ اِنَّ شَانِئَكَ هُوَ الْاَبْتَرُ ۞

In the name of Allah, the All-Merciful, the All-Compassionate
108.1. We have surely granted you (unceasing) abundant good;
108.2. So pray to your Lord, and sacrifice (for Him in thankfulness).
108.3. Surely it is the one who offends you who is cut off (from unceasing good, including posterity).

SURAH AL-KAFIRUN

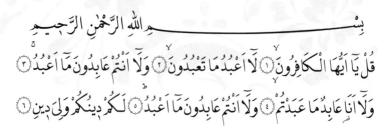

In the name of Allah, the All-Merciful, the All-Compassionate

109.1. Say: "O you unbelievers (who obstinately reject faith)!

109.2. "I do not, nor ever will, worship that which you worship.

109.3. "Nor are you those who ever worship what I worship.

109.4. "Nor am I one who do (and will) ever worship that which you have ever worshipped.

109.5. "And nor are you those who do and will ever worship what I ever worship.

109.6. "You have your religion (with whatever it will bring you), and I have my religion (with whatever it will bring me).

SURAH AN-NASR

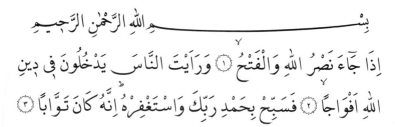

In the name of Allah, the All-Merciful, the All-Compassionate

110.1. When Allah's help comes, and victory,

110.2. And you see people entering Allah's Religion in throngs,

110.3. Then glorify your Lord with His praise, and ask Him for forgiveness; for He surely is One Who returns repentance with liberal forgiveness and additional reward.

AL-MASAD

بِسْمِ اللهِ الرَّحْمٰنِ الرَّحِيمِ

تَبَّتْ يَدَآ اَبِى لَهَبٍ وَّتَبَّ ۝ مَآ اَغْنٰى عَنْهُ مَالُهُ وَمَا كَسَبَ ۝ سَيَصْلٰى نَارًا ذَاتَ لَهَبٍ ۝ وَامْرَاَتُهُ حَمَّالَةَ الْحَطَبِ ۝ فِى جِيدِهَا حَبْلٌ مِّنْ مَّسَدٍ ۝

In the name of Allah, the All-Merciful, the All-Compassionate
111.1. May both hands of Abu Lahab be ruined, and ruined are they!
111.2. His wealth has not availed him, nor his gains.
111.3. He will enter a flaming Fire to roast;
111.4. And (with him) his wife, carrier of firewood (and of evil tales and slander),
111.5. Around her neck will be a halter of strongly twisted rope.

SURAH AL-IKHLAS

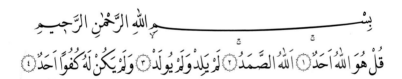

بِسْمِ اللهِ الرَّحْمٰنِ الرَّحِيمِ

قُلْ هُوَ اللهُ اَحَدٌ ۝ اَللهُ الصَّمَدُ ۝ لَمْ يَلِدْ وَلَمْ يُولَدْ ۝ وَلَمْ يَكُنْ لَّهُ كُفُوًا اَحَدٌ ۝

In the name of Allah, the All-Merciful, the All-Compassionate
112.1. Say: "He – (He is) Allah, (Who is) the Unique One of Absolute Oneness.
112.2. "Allah – (Allah is He Who is) the Eternally-Besought-of-All (Himself in no need of anything).
112.3. "He begets not, nor is He begotten.
112.4. "And comparable to Him there is none."

SURAH AL-FALAQ

بِسْمِ اللهِ الرَّحْمٰنِ الرَّحِيمِ

قُلْ اَعُوذُ بِرَبِّ الْفَلَقِ ۟ مِنْ شَرِّ مَا خَلَقَ ۟ وَمِنْ شَرِّ غَاسِقٍ اِذَا وَقَبَ ۟

وَمِنْ شَرِّ النَّفَّاثَاتِ فِى الْعُقَدِ ۟ وَمِنْ شَرِّ حَاسِدٍ اِذَا حَسَدَ ۟

In the name of Allah, the All-Merciful, the All-Compassionate

113.1. Say: "I seek refuge in the Lord of the daybreak

113.2. "From the evil of what He has created;

113.3. "And from the evil of the darkness (of night) when it over-spreads;

113.4. "And from the evil of the witches who blow on knots (to cast a spell);

113.5. "And from the evil of the envious one when he envies."

AN-NAS

بِسْمِ اللهِ الرَّحْمٰنِ الرَّحِيمِ

قُلْ اَعُوذُ بِرَبِّ النَّاسِ ۟ مَلِكِ النَّاسِ ۟ اِلٰهِ النَّاسِ ۟ مِنْ

شَرِّ الْوَسْوَاسِ الْخَنَّاسِ ۟ الَّذِى يُوَسْوِسُ فِى صُدُورِ النَّاسِ ۟

مِنَ الْجِنَّةِ وَالنَّاسِ ۟

In the name of Allah, the All-Merciful, the All-Compassionate

114.1. Say: "I seek refuge in the Lord of humankind,

114.2. "The Sovereign of humankind,

114.3. "The Deity of humankind,

114.4. "From the evil of the sneaking whisperer (the Satan),

114.5. "Who whispers into the hearts of humankind,

114.6. "Of the jinn and humankind."

AYAT'UL-KURSI (FROM *SURAH AL-BAQARAH*)

بِسْمِ اللهِ الرَّحْمٰنِ الرَّحِيمِ

اَللهُ لَا اِلٰهَ اِلَّا هُوَ اَلْحَيُّ الْقَيُّومُ لَا تَأْخُذُهُ سِنَةٌ وَّلَا نَوْمٌ لَهُ مَا فِى السَّمٰوَاتِ وَمَا فِى الْاَرْضِ مَنْ ذَا الَّذِى يَشْفَعُ عِنْدَهُ اِلَّا بِاِذْنِهِ يَعْلَمُ مَا بَيْنَ اَيْدِيهِمْ وَمَا خَلْفَهُمْ وَلَا يُحِيطُونَ بِشَىْءٍ مِنْ عِلْمِهِ اِلَّا بِمَا شَاءَ وَسِعَ كُرْسِيُّهُ السَّمٰوَاتِ وَالْاَرْضَ وَلَا يَؤُدُهُ حِفْظُهُمَا وَهُوَ الْعَلِىُّ الْعَظِيمُ ۝

In the name of Allah, the All-Merciful, the All-Compassionate 2.255. Allah, there is no deity but He; the All-Living, the Self-Subsisting (by Whom all subsist). Slumber does not seize Him, nor sleep. His is all that is in the heavens and all that is on the earth. Who is there that will intercede with Him save by His leave? He knows what lies before them and what lies after them (what lies in their future and in their past, what is known to them and what is hidden from them); and they do not comprehend anything of His Knowledge save what He wills. His Seat (of dominion) embraces the heavens and the earth, and the preserving of them does not weary Him; He is the All-Exalted, the Supreme.

HUVALLAHULLAZI
(FROM THE SURAH AL-HASHR)

بِسْمِ اللهِ الرَّحْمٰنِ الرَّحِيمِ

هُوَ اللهُ الَّذِى لَا اِلٰهَ اِلَّا هُوَ عَالِمُ الْغَيْبِ وَالشَّهَادَةِ هُوَ الرَّحْمٰنُ الرَّحِيمُ ۝ هُوَ اللهُ الَّذِى لَا اِلٰهَ اِلَّا هُوَ اَلْمَلِكُ الْقُدُّوسُ السَّلَامُ الْمُؤْمِنُ الْمُهَيْمِنُ الْعَزِيزُ الْجَبَّارُ الْمُتَكَبِّرُ سُبْحَانَ اللهِ عَمَّا يُشْرِكُونَ ۝ هُوَ اللهُ الْخَالِقُ الْبَارِئُ الْمُصَوِّرُ لَهُ الْاَسْمَاءُ الْحُسْنٰى يُسَبِّحُ لَهُ مَا فِى السَّمٰوَاتِ وَالْاَرْضِ وَهُوَ الْعَزِيزُ الْحَكِيمُ ۝

In the name of Allah, the All-Merciful, the All-Compassionate

59.22. Allah is He save Whom there is no deity: the Knower of the unseen (all that lies beyond sense-perception), and the witnessed (the sensed realm). He is the All-Merciful, the All-Compassionate.

59.23. Allah is He save Whom there is no deity: the Sovereign, the All-Holy and All-Pure, the Supreme Author of peace and salvation, and the Supreme Author of safety and security Who bestows faith and removes all doubt, the All-Watchful Guardian, the All-Glorious with irresistible might, the All-Compelling of supreme majesty, the One Who has exclusive right to all greatness. All-Glorified is Allah in that He is absolutely exalted above what they associate with Him.

59.24. He is Allah, the Creator, the All-Holy Maker (Who creates without any defects), the All-Fashioning. To Him belong the All-Beautiful Names. Whatever is in the heavens and on the earth glorifies Him (declaring Him to be absolutely above having any defects). He is the All-Glorious with irresistible might, the All-Wise.

THE PRAYERS

AL-ISTIFTAH PRAYER OR SUBHANAKA PRAYER (SUPPLICATION OF STARTING)

سُبْحَانَكَ اللّٰهُمَّ وَبِحَمْدِكَ ۞ وَتَبَارَكَ اسْمُكَ ۞ وَتَعَالَى جَدُّكَ ۞ (وَجَلَّ ثَنَاؤُكَ) وَلَا اِلٰهَ غَيْرُكَ ۞

Glory be to You, O Allah, and to You is the praise. Blessed is Your Name. And most high is Your honor. And Your praise is glorified (read only in a funeral prayer). There is no deity besides You.

AT-TASHAHUD OR AT-TAHIYYATU PRAYER

اَلتَّحِيَّاتُ لِلّٰهِ وَالصَّلَوَاتُ وَالطَّيِّبَاتُ ۞ اَلسَّلَامُ عَلَيْكَ اَيُّهَا النَّبِيُّ وَرَحْمَةُ اللّٰهِ وَبَرَكَاتُهُ ۞ اَلسَّلَامُ عَلَيْنَا وَعَلَى عِبَادِ اللّٰهِ الصَّالِحِينَ ۞ اَشْهَدُ اَنْ لَاَ اِلٰهَ اِلاَّ اللّٰهُ ۞ وَاَشْهَدُ اَنَّ مُحَمَّدًا عَبْدُهُ وَرَسُولُهُ ۞

All the worship, prayers and goodness [performed by all living creatures through their lives] are for Allah. Peace be upon you O the [greatest] Prophet, and Allah's mercy and gifts. Peace be also upon us and Allah's righteous servants. I bear witness that there is no deity but Allah, and I also bear witness that Muhammad is His servant and Messenger.

ALLAHUMMA SALLI PRAYER

اَللّٰهُمَّ صَلِّ عَلَى سَيِّدِنَا مُحَمَّدٍ وَعَلَى اٰلِ سَيِّدِنَا مُحَمَّدٍ ⦿ كَمَا صَلَّيْتَ عَلَى سَيِّدِنَا إِبْرٰهِيمَ ⦿ وَعَلَى اٰلِ سَيِّدِنَا إِبْرٰهِيمَ ⦿ اِنَّكَ حَمِيدٌ مَجِيدٌ ⦿

O Allah, bestow Your blessings upon our master Muhammad and the Family of Muhammad, as You bestowed Your blessings upon Abraham and the Family of Abraham. Assuredly, You are All-Praised, All-Illustrious.

ALLAHUMMA BARIK PRAYER

اَللّٰهُمَّ بَارِكْ عَلَى سَيِّدِنَا مُحَمَّدٍ وَعَلَى اٰلِ سَيِّدِنَا مُحَمَّدٍ ⦿ كَمَا بَارَكْتَ عَلَى سَيِّدِنَا إِبْرٰهِيمَ وَعَلَى اٰلِ سَيِّدِنَا إِبْرٰهِيمَ ⦿ اِنَّكَ حَمِيدٌ مَجِيدٌ ⦿

O Allah, send Your abundant gifts and favors unto our master Muhammad and the Family of Muhammad, as You sent them unto Abraham and the Family of Abraham. Assuredly, You are All-Praised, All-Illustrious.

RABBANA PRAYER

رَبَّنَا اٰتِنَا فِي الدُّنْيَا حَسَنَةً وَفِي الْاٰخِرَةِ حَسَنَةً وَقِنَا عَذَابَ النَّارِ ۞ رَبَّنَا اغْفِرْ لِي وَلِوَالِدَيَّ وَلِلْمُؤْمِنِينَ يَوْمَ يَقُومُ الْحِسَابُ ۞

O our Lord! Grant us goodness in this world and in the Hereafter and protect us from the punishment of the fire.

O our Lord! Grant forgiveness to me when the Final Day of Judgment comes, and to my parents and to the believers.

QUNUT PRAYER - 1

اَللّٰهُمَّ إِنَّا نَسْتَعِينُكَ وَنَسْتَغْفِرُكَ وَنَسْتَهْدِيكَ ۞ وَنُؤْمِنُ بِكَ وَنَتَوَكَّلُ عَلَيْكَ ۞ وَنُثْنِي عَلَيْكَ الْخَيْرَ كُلَّهُ ۞ نَشْكُرُكَ وَلَا نَكْفُرُكَ ۞ وَنَخْلَعُ وَنَتْرُكُ مَنْ يَفْجُرُكَ ۞

O Allah! We ask You for help, forgiveness, and guidance. We believe in You and turn to You in repentance for our sins, and place our trust in You. We praise You by attributing all good to You, and thank You, and never feel ingratitude to You. We reject and cut our relations with those who are in constant rebellion against You.

QUNUT PRAYER - 2

اَللّٰهُمَّ اِيَّاكَ نَعْبُدُ ⬤ ولَكَ نُصَلِّي وَنَسْجُدُ ⬤
وَإِلَيْكَ نَسْعَى وَنحْفِدُ ⬤ نَرْجُو رَحْمَتَكَ وَنَخْشَى
عَذَابَكَ ⬤ اِنَّ عَذَابَكَ بِالْكُفَّارِ مُلْحِقٌ ⬤

O Allah, You alone do we worship, and we pray and prostrate for You alone. We endeavor in Your way to obtain Your good pleasure and approval. We hope and expect Your Mercy and fear Your chastisement, for Your chastisement is to surround the unbelievers.

PRAYER MADE FOR SUCCESS

My Lord, make my task easy for me and not make it difficult, and My Lord, end it with goodness.

PRAYER FOR PARENTS

My Lord, have mercy on my parents even as they cared for me in childhood.

PRAYER AFTER MEALS

All praise is due to Allah who gave us food and drink and who made us Muslims.